BUILDING WORLD LANDMARKS

The CN Tower

by Meg Greene

**BLACKBIRCH®
PRESS**

THOMSON
™
GALE

San Diego • Detroit • New York • San Francisco • Cleveland • New Haven, Conn. • Waterville, Maine • London • Munich

Table of Contents

The Tallest Tower in the World

ONE OF HUMANKIND'S greatest accomplishments is the ability to build tall structures. The idea that one could build something that soared toward the skies has always captured people's imaginations. Building tall structures has always posed a great challenge. Throughout history, humans have met that test in a variety of ways.

Tall structures can include monuments and buildings. Another example of a tall structure is a tower, which by definition is a structure that is higher than it is wide. Towers can be one of two types. The first kind of tower is symbolic; that is, it represents something. The second type of tower is more practical in nature and serves a specific purpose. Within these two basic types are a wide variety of towers.

The first type of tower, dating back to the earliest civilizations, was built to represent the power and authority of various religious groups. One early example is the ziggurats built in ancient Mesopotamia beginning around 3000 B.C. Built out of sun-dried bricks,

Opposite:
The CN Tower is the tallest freestanding structure in the world.

5

the ziggurats are large, stepped, pyramid-shaped structures that were used for worship. The architects of the ziggurats, the Sumerians, placed these large towers in the center of their cities.

In India, pyramidal and cylindrical towers were built as decoration for religious temples. In China and Japan, pagodas built of timber or brick, which stand several stories high with gently sloping roofs, were used as Buddhist temples. In western Europe during the Middle Ages, the towers and spires of the great cathedrals rose majestically to the skies. Even in colonial America, many New England towns had a distinctive church with a small wooden tower and steeple rising directly over the entrance doors.

The second type of tower served more practical purposes. Some towers were built for defense, such as those attached to fortress castles. Towers such as the campanile in Renaissance Italy were built to hold bells near a church. Lighthouses, which date back to the Egyptians, were used to warn ships of land or water dangers. With the arrival of modern technology such as electricity in the nineteenth and twentieth centuries, more sophisticated towers were built for use as beacons or signal towers, or as communications antennae, one example of which is the grand Eiffel Tower in Paris.

Some of the greatest towers built in the twentieth century have taken the form of skyscrapers. These buildings consist of a

People have been building towers for thousands of years. Pagodas in China and Japan, such as this one, were used as Buddhist temples.

metal framework or skeleton that is enclosed with glass or other lightweight material. This method allows buildings to be very high, so high that they appear to touch the sky. Some examples of skyscrapers include the Empire State Building in New York City; the unusual Einstein Tower at Potsdam, Germany; the Sears Tower in Chicago; and the Petronas Towers in Kuala Lumpur, Malaysia.

As building technology improves, architects and engineers compete to build the tallest building in the world. For many years, the tallest tower in the world was the Eiffel Tower, which stands 990 feet (300 meters) high. Many newer towers have held the title of tallest tower in the world. Today, that honor belongs to the CN Tower.

The Eiffel Tower was, for many years, the tallest tower in the world.

The CN Tower is the most recognizable landmark in Toronto, Canada's largest city. The tower, which stands 1,815 feet (553.35 meters) high, is the tallest freestanding structure in the world. It surpasses Moscow's Ostankino state broadcasting tower at 1,771 feet (540 meters) and the Taipei 101 in Taipei, Taiwan, the world's tallest office building, which stands 1,667 feet (508 meters) high. The CN Tower is considered freestanding because it has no need of guy wires, or special supports to hold it straight and steady. The tower is also impressive architecturally and an engineering wonder. It is the source of great pride not only for the residents of Toronto, but for Canadians everywhere.

A Very Big Idea

DURING THE BUILDING boom in Toronto, Canada, in the late 1960s and early 1970s, a serious communications problem developed. People began experiencing poor television reception. The new taller buildings that dominated the cityscape were so high that the signals sent by the transmission towers of Toronto television stations literally bounced off them. This caused all kinds of annoyances for television viewers. The most common problem, the collision of weaker signals with stronger ones, caused something called "ghosting," in which the television appeared to be broadcasting two programs at once. Even listening to the radio was a challenge because static drowned out radio programs.

Seeking a Solution

In 1972, Canadian National Railways (CN), a historic railway and telegraph company, proposed building a

Opposite:
As tall buildings rose all over Toronto, people began to have problems with radio and television reception because transmission signals bounced off the buildings.

The CN Tower was initially supposed to be part of Metro Centre, a large building project that would require the demolition of Toronto's historic Union Station (pictured).

tower that would solve the reception problems. The CN Tower was to be part of a larger building project called the Metro Centre, scheduled to be built on 190 acres of railway land no longer used by the company in downtown Toronto. The proposal for the Metro Centre included office buildings, shops, apartments, and condominiums, along with the broadcasting tower.

It soon became clear, however, that the Metro Centre project was doomed. To build the Centre meant demolishing Union Station, one of Toronto's best-known landmarks. So many people were against the planned destruction of the building that in the end, the proposed complex was cancelled.

The tower idea though, would not die. Norman MacMillan, head of the CN board, made it clear that no matter what, he would build a tower on the company's property. As soon as CN Railways received approval to build on the land, work got under way.

The Experts Come In

To design and build the tower, Canadian National Railways hired two architectural firms. The design for the tower was created by Australian architect John Andrews and his firm John Andrews Architects, based in Toronto. In designing the CN Tower, Andrews was originally more interested in producing a design that

Eventually, the CN Tower was built at this site near Lake Ontario, in the middle of rail yards that were no longer used.

fit in with the tower's proposed location and that would serve the telecommunications needs of the tower, rather than with creating a structure with a distinctive style. It was not until much later in the design process that the design team decided to turn the tower into a tourist attraction as well.

The CN Tower was to be built in the middle of no longer used rail yards situated near Lake Ontario. The original design plan for the tower featured not just one, but three, towers to be linked together by bridges. The final design consisted of a single tower with three tall, hollow "legs," or supports. Sitting atop the legs would be a radome, a collarlike structure that would house telecommunications equipment. Directly above the radome would be a seven-story structure. This area would not only provide visitors with the opportunity to view the scenic vista from the tower, but would provide additional revenue as a tourist attraction by including restaurants and other features such as gift and souvenir shops. Above this structure, the tower would extend another estimated four hundred feet in concrete. This area would serve as a base for the tower's 335-foot (102-meter) metal antenna and would also include the Sky Pod, another observation deck for visitors. The vast majority of the tower would be constructed using the most superior kind of concrete available.

To anchor the tower's legs, a Y-shaped foundation of prestressed concrete, reinforced steel, and thick steel cables would be created. This man-made foundation would rest on a shale base. To support the

An Amazing Feat

Just before construction of the tower began, labor statistics predicted that given the size of the construction crew, there would be at least a dozen deaths. There was, in fact, only one. A piece of plywood whipped about by the wind killed an outside consultant while he was taking measurements. The speed and force of the wind was such that the plywood broke the man's neck. There was only one other close call. During construction, a worker dropped several 4.5- to 5.5-inch (11.5- to 14-centimeter) bolts off the top where he was working. The force of the bolts traveling down could have seriously injured someone. Miraculously, no one was hurt.

Despite predictions of at least a dozen deaths, only one person was killed during construction of the CN Tower.

tower's size, the legs and the foundation would have to be set far into the ground. The team's engineers determined that this was necessary if the tower was to stand straight and steady.

Landscaping of the tower grounds was also an important consideration. Planners decided that a parklike setting would be the most inviting. The grounds surrounding the tower area would be terraced and slope toward a large reflecting pool that would surround the base of the tower. Because of the large, green, open space, the area would draw people not only to visit the tower, but to walk the grounds in good weather.

The Team Begins Work

To help oversee the project was architect Ned Baldwin of the Webb Zerafa Menkes Housden Partnership,

Before working on the CN Tower project, the team members had little experience with tall structures. Gund Hall (pictured) is an earlier project by John Andrews Architects.

who would work together with the firm of John Andrews. Baldwin ended up on the project only because his firm had been promised work when the plans for the Metro Centre were first under way, not because he had experience building tall buildings. In fact, Baldwin, before being assigned to the CN Tower project, had never built anything higher than six stories. Only one person on the team had ever built a tall structure, and that was a chimney.

The first important question facing the team was how deep to set the tower's foundation into the ground so the structure would be as stable and secure as possible. To determine this, an elaborate series of tests were performed on the soil. First, tests were done to assess the condition of the bedrock. Then the engineers had to evaluate how the bedrock would stand up to any changes as a result of the construction. A team of geology graduate students from the University of Toronto helped the engineers carry out the tests. The students were lowered down a number of deep test holes, three hundred feet deep and three feet wide, that had been drilled by the construction crew that was to dig the foundation. They then offered their calculations to the engineers based on their findings in the test holes. After studying the calculations along with their own, the engineers decided that the proposed 1,500-foot (457-meter) tower could be anchored by digging only fifty feet (15.25 meters) into the ground. Now the tower's construction could begin.

Chapter 2

The Tower Takes Shape

FINALLY CAME THE day everyone was waiting for. On February 6, 1973, hundreds of workers began to build the tower. The design team decided to go ahead and lay the foundation even before the tower's design was finalized. They realized that, as they had on many other building projects, they would be designing and redesigning as needed during the construction to make sure the tower was as safe and sturdy as possible.

Building the Foundation

To prepare the foundation, giant backhoes removed more than 62,000 tons (55,800 metric tons) of earth and shale to create a 50-foot- (15.25-meter-) deep, Y-shaped hole. At the bottom of the hole was the shale and earth that would provide the base for the tower's foundation. After the shale base was smoothed by hand and machine, the next step was the installation

Opposite:
Construction on the tower began in early 1973, before its design was finalized.

17

More than sixty-two thousand tons of earth and shale were removed to create a fifty-foot hole for the tower's Y-shape foundation.

of a 22-foot- (7-meter-) thick, Y-shaped pattern mold into the hole. Into this form, prestressed concrete and reinforced steel were arranged on top of the shale base.

This Y-shape foundation would support each of the three hollow legs of the tower. The foundation would also equally distribute the 130,000-ton (117,000-metric-ton) weight of the finished tower. When it was finally completed, the foundation contained 9,200 cubic yards (7,034 cubic meters) of concrete, 500 tons (450 metric tons) of reinforcing steel, and 40 tons (36 metric tons) of thick, tensioning cables which would help maintain the Y shape of the form.

The foundation was not only breathtaking in its size, the speed in which workers completed it was also remarkable: Only four months after the groundbreaking, the finished foundation was in place. Now the construction team turned their attention to building the parts of the structure that would be aboveground.

Here, the team faced many unknowns. For instance, there were questions about how to construct the observation deck located in the Sky Pod area. Another question was how best to lift the pieces used to build the tower as it rose higher and higher. To solve this problem, the team decided to use a large crane to hoist the tower's pieces to and from the ground.

Building the Shaft

Once the foundation was ready, work began on the CN Tower's 1,100-foot (335-meter) concrete shaft. The three concrete legs would have hollow hexagonal centers and would surround the central shaft, which

This photo shows the view down the CN Tower's central shaft. Workers poured concrete twenty-four hours a day, five days a week, to build the hexagonal shaft.

would also be hollow. This center was where the tower's electrical cables and water piping would be placed. To construct the shaft, designers made use of a construction technique known as a "slipform," which

On February 22, 1974, a year after construction began, workers poured the last concrete at the top of the tower.

had been developed in Sweden. This process involved pouring concrete into a massive, doughnut-shaped mold, or slipform, that the engineers had designed. When the concrete was hardened and dry, the mold would slowly be moved upward, where more concrete would be poured. As the slipform moved upward, the tower would take shape.

The slipform was supported by a circle of climbing jacks, portable pieces of machinery used to move heavy objects short distances at a time. The jacks, powered by hydraulic pressure, moved the slipform upward. The hardened concrete below the form also helped to support the mold as the jacks slowly pushed the form up. To give the tower a graceful tapered shape, the shaft and the form began gradually decreasing in size as the tower rose.

To construct the tower shaft, construction workers worked in shifts, so that concrete could be poured twenty-four hours a day, five days a week. To maintain consistency, the construction team made sure that all the concrete came from the same source. Workers mixed all of the concrete on-site, testing and retesting it to make sure that the concrete mixture was all the same.

Standing Tall and Straight

To check that the shaft was staying plumb, or straight, the engineers used aircraft-type bombsights, a type of sighting device typically used by airplane pilots to target potential bombing positions. The sights allowed the engineers to check the tower construction from hundreds of feet away and make sure that the tower stood straight as it went up.

Slowly, the tower's shaft, which rose by twenty-four feet each day, started to take shape. When the shaft was completed, there were a number of horizontal bands throughout. They became known as "Friday Lines" because they marked where the workers had stopped pouring concrete for the weekend.

The Observation Pod

Once the tower reached 1,100 feet (335 meters), the builders turned their attention to the construction of the Observation Pod. The proposed structure was to

A Tower of a Different Color

Long after the CN Tower's completion, one of the project's directors stated in an interview that the now familiar landmark was almost painted pink. During the tower's construction, a member of the design committee suggested that a pink dye be mixed with the concrete to cover the tower's dull gray color. The majority of the design team quickly voiced their objections, and the idea was vetoed.

be seven stories high, and would house not only broadcasting equipment but a variety of attractions including two observation decks, a revolving restaurant, and a nightclub.

The Observation Pod itself was built with concrete walls. Before construction of the pod began, materials identical to those to be used on the Observation Pod

The Observation Pod was built on the ground and forty-five hydraulic jacks raised it into place more than eleven hundred feet above the ground.

were subjected to rigorous lab tests using furnace flames to check for fire safety. The tests revealed that the pod would have to burn for two hours before the structure was in any danger of collapsing. The Observation Pod was built on the ground at the base of the

All of the tower's sensitive microwave communication dishes are housed in the doughnut-shaped structure under the Observation Pod.

tower. To raise the structure, 350 tons (318 metric tons) of steel and wood brackets were built to anchor the Observation Pod and protect it from falling. Then with the help of forty-five hydraulic jacks, the Observation Pod was raised up to its final destination 1,150 feet (350.5 meters) above ground. There, the jacks secured the structure in place.

Underneath the base of the Observation Pod, the team placed a doughnut-shaped collar known as a radome. Here all of the sensitive microwave communication dishes would be located, shielded from the weather. The incoming radio and television transmission signals would be sent here and then fed to the antenna on top of the tower. The radome's balloonlike look came about as the result of inflating its specially teflon-coated fiberglass rayon fabric skin to five times its normal size, then maintaining a constant air pressure to keep the skin's shape. In addition, four high-speed, glass-fronted elevators were installed that would take people to and from the Observation Pod area.

After the completion of the Observation Pod, the next step was to build the concrete base for the tower's antenna. The base also featured the Sky Pod, which would have another observation deck, one that stood 1,465 feet (446.5 meters) above ground and completely encircled the antenna base. To support the Sky Pod and prevent it from collapsing, special cantilevers, or projecting beams, were angled to the bottom of the deck and attached to the wall of the base. Finally, another sixteen feet of concrete base was built, on top of which the tower's antenna would be placed.

Reaching Even Higher

As THE CN Tower rose, the architects and engineers kept making modifications to the design. At one point it was discovered that the design would not be able to house all the radio stations that wanted to be included. The problem was solved with the addition of another floor to the Observation Pod.

The architects also faced another problem. According to the design, there would be large areas of the tower surface that could not be easily reached in the future. This meant that if there was a problem with the outside surface of the structure, no one would be able to reach the area to take care of it. Ned Baldwin and his team recognized that by making changes in the design such as adding special rigging, or supports, in fact most of the tower could be reached if needed.

Opposite:
While the Observation Pod was being built, designers realized that the CN Tower would be the world's tallest freestanding tower if they added another one hundred feet.

Until the CN Tower was built, the Ostankino Tower (pictured) in Moscow was the tallest in the world.

Taking a Chance

During the building of the Observation Pod, the tower's design team realized that if they added a little more height to the tower it could become the world's tallest freestanding tower. The team went to Norman MacMillan and explained that with the addition of approximately 100 feet (30.5 meters), the CN Tower would not only be the tallest tower in Toronto or Canada but would also beat out the 1,771-foot (540-meter) Ostankino Tower in Moscow, Russia, as the tallest in the world.

MacMillan agreed, in part because of the challenge. He also saw an opportunity to beat the Russians by doing something better. During this period political tensions between the Soviet Union and the West saw both regions competing against each other in everything from space travel to developing the latest in nuclear weaponry. With CN's consent, the designers lengthened that shaft between the Observation Pod and the Sky Pod roughly 100 feet (30.5 meters) to achieve the desired height.

The Antenna

The last thing to be added to the tower was the 335-foot (102-meter) steel broadcasting antenna. The antenna consisted of more than forty pieces, each 5 feet (1.5 meters) in diameter. All the pieces but one weighed 7 tons (6.5 metric tons), with the remaining piece weighing approximately 8 tons (7.2 metric tons). Before the antenna could be put into place, the giant crane, which had been used to hoist materials and was located where the antenna would be placed, would have to be taken apart and brought down.

Instead of using a crane to build the antenna on top of the tower, a helicopter lifted the pieces into place, drastically cutting construction time and costs.

To complete this last phase of construction, the design team hired a firm in California to send them a special kind of helicopter and trained crew to help with placement of the antenna. With the aid of the helicopter, the time needed to complete this last phase of construction would be cut drastically. The team figured that if the building of the antenna was done by a construction crew and crane, it would take six months. Doing the job by helicopter, however, would take only three weeks. This would lower construction costs by thousands of dollars.

In early spring, the crew of four flew to Toronto to begin work. At the time, the Americans knew that this was their biggest job ever. What they did not realize was that they were about to make history by helping finish the world's tallest structure.

Olga

The four American pilots and mechanics arrived in Toronto with great fanfare. But stealing the show was the crew's helicopter, nicknamed "Olga." The helicopter, a ten-ton (nine-metric-ton) Sikorsky S64 Skycrane, is a special copter used mostly for industrial lifting. A large "Hey, Look me over" sticker on the copter's nose invited people to watch it at work.

But the first time out with Olga, disaster almost struck. As the helicopter was removing the first piece of the crane called the jib boom, the crane swayed, twisted, and got tangled with the support bolts that held the crane to the tower. Try as they might, the crew could not release the crane from Olga. Now hovering

Nicknamed "Olga," the helicopter and her crew of four made fifty-five trips to carry more than forty pieces of the antenna to the top of the tower.

about 1,500 feet (457 meters) up, the helicopter was attached to the crane, which was in turn attached to the tower. Even worse, while the job was estimated to take only twelve minutes, the copter was quickly using up fuel. The crew had estimated the job to take no more than fifty minutes of fuel. If the crew could not free themselves and the helicopter from the tower, the copter would plummet 1,500 feet down and crash. Steel workers scrambled up to the tower and crane. By cutting off the crane's bolts, they were able to release

As each piece of the antenna was brought up, workers stood at the top of the tower, guided it into place, and bolted it to the previous pieces.

the crane from the tower. Olga landed on the ground with only fourteen minutes of fuel left.

As work on taking apart the crane progressed, tower watchers became great fans of Olga and her crew. Every day the helicopter's schedule appeared in the local newspapers, and updates on the tower's progress was broadcast on radio and television. Olga became a big favorite with the design team, too.

Finally it was time to assemble the antenna. Lifting one piece at a time, Olga carried the more than forty

pieces of the antenna to the top of the tower. As each piece of antenna was raised, workers would stand at the top and help maneuver it into place. They then installed the pieces. The pieces were secured with a total of more than forty thousand bolts. The conditions of the antenna assembly were brutal. Even though it was early spring, heavy winds and freezing temperatures made working conditions dangerous.

On April 2, 1975, after more than three and a half weeks of heavy work, the final piece of antenna was secured. It took Olga fifty-five trips to complete the building of the antenna. The last section was particularly special; local children had been invited to sign their names on it. But even as the final piece of was being lifted into place, there was a tense moment. The final section of the antenna had been hooked on backward, and the workers had to turn the piece around before putting it in place. The high rigger, working without safety ropes and battling the downdraft from Olga's blade, finally set the last piece in place onto the tower. The finished mast was then covered with a special sheathing that would make it difficult for ice to form on the antenna. In addition, a pair of ten-ton counterweights was attached to the antenna to keep the tower from swaying too much.

City residents watched the sight from office towers, from the area around the tower, even from their cars on the Gardiner Expressway. As people below clapped and cheered, the Canadian flag was unfolded and began waving in the wind. The CN Tower was finished. It was an amazing sight and an unforgettable moment.

Chapter 4

Television Tower to Tourist Attraction

AFTER FORTY MONTHS of construction, the CN Tower was opened to the public on June 26, 1976. Four months later, on October 1, 1976, a formal dedication of the tower was held. Helping to commemorate the event were the Canadian minister of finance, acting on behalf of Canadian prime minister Pierre Trudeau; various city and provincial officials; members of the design team; and of course, hundreds of ordinary citizens. Already, the tower was well on its way to becoming not just Toronto's, but Canada's most celebrated landmark.

A Look Inside

Visitors to the CN Tower can enjoy a number of different attractions on the four levels of the tower, including the Sky Pod. The first stop for visitors is the Entrance Building, which is a one-story building

Opposite:
The more than 2 million people who visit the CN Tower each year enjoy the numerous attractions it offers as one of Toronto's most celebrated landmarks.

The Glass Floor is made of two-and-a-half-inch-thick glass panels and is so strong that it could hold fourteen large hippos.

attached to the tower. Here information about the tower, gift and souvenir shops, and a restaurant are located. A digital weather display provides information. People then move on to the tower base which offers a restaurant, lounge, and arcade. Tickets for the observation decks can be purchased here. To visit the upper levels of the tower, visitors can take an elevator. The elevators are covered with glass on three sides and move quickly, traveling at a rate of fifteen mph, or twelve hundred feet a minute. Some visitors have compared the speedy elevator ride to that of a jet plane taking off from a runway.

The lowest level, at a height of 1,122 feet (342 meters), contains the Glass Floor and Outdoor Observation Deck. The Glass Floor was specially designed for the CN Tower. The 256-square-foot (23-square meter) floor is made of solid glass panels measuring 42 inches (1 meter) by 50 inches (1.5 meters) each; each panel is 2.5 inches (6.3 centimeters) thick. Each floor panel consists of two .5-inch (1.25-centimeter) layers of clear tempered glass laminated together along with a 1-inch (2.5-centimeter) layer of air for insulation and two .25-inch (.6-centimeter) layers of clear tempered glass. Covering the entire glass floor is a scuff plate, which consists of a large piece of clear plexiglass. The scuff plate provides a protective covering that helps reduce the scratches and scuffs on the floor's surface. The plate is replaced every year. The glass floor is five times stronger than the required weight for commercial

Pictured here is the view through the CN Tower's Glass Floor, through which hundreds of visitors take photos every year.

floors, and tests are performed annually on each panel to ensure safety. In fact, the floor is so strong, it has been estimated that it could actually hold the weight of fourteen large hippos.

The second level of the tower, known as Look Out Level, stands 1,136 feet (346 meters) aboveground and features an indoor observation deck, a restaurant, theaters, and gift and souvenir shops. Another elevator ride takes people to the third level, where one can view a full 360-degree unobstructed view of the Toronto City skyline from 1,150 feet (250.5 meters) aboveground. Also at this level is a revolving restaurant; diners get a complete view of the city below during the seventy-two minutes it takes for the restaurant to rotate. For those wishing to brave even higher heights, there is the fourth level, the Sky Pod, the World's Highest Public Observation Deck, stands a dizzying 1,465 feet (447 meters) aboveground.

Some Amazing Facts

In the end, the total cost to build the CN tower was $63 million, approximately $300 million in today's dollars. Experts believe that it would be almost impossible to build a tower of this size today because of the immense cost. The ambitious project involved 1,537 workers. Work went on around the clock, five days a week for forty months. The CN measures roughly the height of five and a half football fields stacked lengthwise. It weighs 130,000 tons (117,910 metric tons), which is twice as heavy as the world's biggest luxury liner and about the same weight as 23,214 large

The CN Tower Time Capsule

Not long after the tower's formal opening, a time capsule was placed into the tower. Included in the capsule was a letter from Pierre Trudeau, then prime minister of Canada; letters of congratulation from each of the provincial premiers (similar to U.S. governors), and letters about the tower from schoolchildren all over Canada. Also placed inside the capsule were copies of the three daily newspapers, the *Toronto Star*, the *Toronto Sun*, and the *Globe and Mail*. Canadian coins and bills of various denominations were also tucked in, as was a copy of the video *To The Top*, which describes the tower's construction. The capsule was placed inside the walls of the tower on Look Out Level. The official opening of the time capsule will take place in the year 2076.

Canadian prime minister Pierre Trudeau was one of the many people who wrote letters that were included in the CN Tower time capsule.

The CN Tower, which is the height of five and a half football fields stacked lengthwise, took more than fifteen hundred workers and $63 million to build.

elephants. 53,000 cubic yards (40,521 cubic meters) of concrete were poured to build the tower. This is enough concrete to build a curb that would run from Toronto to Kingston, Ontario, 150 miles (241 km) away. With 1,760 steps, the tower's metal staircase is the largest in the world.

Even though the tower can withstand wind gusts as high as 260 mph (241 km/h), on a windy day, the tower can still sway by as much as 7 feet (2 meters). In winds of 120 mph (193 km/h), with 200 mph (322 km/h) gusts, the antenna sways a little over 6 feet (1.8 meters); the Sky Pod, approximately 3 feet (1 meter); and the Observation Pod, about 1 foot (30 centimeters). The tower is also an easy target for lightning hits. To prevent damage to the tower from lightning, engineers had copper grounding wires installed. Still, one of the great sights for people visiting the tower on a stormy day is the chance to see the actual lightning strikes to the structure.

Roughly 2 million people visit the CN Tower every year. Approximately 400 people work in the tower, though during peak seasons that number increases to 550 people. The tower has also been the site of some strange stunts such as the highest egg-dropping contest. People have also carried pumpkins to the observation deck, with the idea of dropping them to the ground. People have also ridden motorbikes up the stairs. One construction worker smuggled a parachute to the top of the tower and jumped down. The tower has also been a fashionable place for parties and weddings. Walking the tower's steps has also been a popular way for charity groups to raise money.

In 2001, two Greenpeace activists climbed the outside of the tower and hung a banner to protest the inaction of Canada and the United States in protecting the environment.

Records of All Kinds

Besides being the tallest freestanding tower in the world, the CN Tower has also been awarded a number of other distinctions. It is noted for having the world's longest metal staircase and the world's highest wine cellar, located in the tower's restaurant, "360," which is 1,150 feet (350.5 meters) above ground. In 1995, the CN Tower was designated as one of the Seven Wonders of the Modern World by the American Society of Civil Engineers. The Tower is listed along with such other famous structures as the Golden Gate Bridge in San Francisco, the Panama Canal, the Chunnel under the English Channel, and the Empire State Building in New York City. In 1996, the CN Tower was classified as the World's Tallest Building and Free-Standing Structure by the Guinness Book of World Records.

Among its many distinctions, the CN Tower has been named one of the Seven Wonders of the Modern World.

Some visitors are not quite sure what the CN Tower is exactly. On more than one occasion, visitors have mistakenly assumed the tower was a hotel and tried to get a room. One tourist was convinced that the tower was really a nuclear launch site and that the hollow shaft contained a giant missile.

The tower is an inspiring sight. It is almost twice the height of the Eiffel Tower and measures more than three times the height of the Washington Monument. Its claim as tallest freestanding structure may be toppled, as newer and taller buildings continue to be built the world over. For those who built the tower and those who live in Toronto, however, the CN Tower is a visible reminder of how humans once again reached for the heavens.

Rising high above the Toronto skyline, the CN Tower is an inspiring site.

Chronology

1972   CN Tower idea approved by Canadian National Railways (CN).

1973   Ground is broken for the tower in February; foundation work is completed by June.

1974   Completion of concrete shaft in February; construction begins on Observation Pod.

1975   Last piece of tower antenna lifted into place, tower completed April 2.

1976   Tower opened to the public June 26.

1995   CN Tower classified as one of the Seven Wonders of the Modern World by the American Society of Civil Engineers.

Glossary

bedrock—Solid rock that lies beneath the soil.

boom—A long pole that extends upward and outward from a crane and supports a lifted object.

hexagonal—Having six sides.

prestressed concrete—Structural concrete in which heavy objects have been placed inside to reduce stress in the concrete.

shaft—An enclosed space extending through one or more levels of a structure.

shale—Rocks consisting of layers of clay and fine particles of sand pressed together.

For More Information

Books

Leslie Allen et al., *The Wonders of the World*. Washington, DC: National Geographic Society, 1998.

CN Tower/La Tour CN. Toronto: Royal Specialty Sales.

Web Sites

CN Tower (www.cntower.ca/default.htm). Official Web site of the CN Tower.

The CN Tower (www.ewh.ieee.org/reg/7/millenium/cntower/cntower_home.html). Provides an overview of the tower's construction.

CN Tower (http://wonderclub.com/WorldWonders/CNTowerHistory.html). Another brief history of the tower's construction.

So You Wanna Know the Ten Tallest Buildings in the World? (www.soyouwanna.com/site/toptens/buildings/buildings.html). A look at how the CN Tower stacks up against other tall buildings.

Welcome to the CN Tower Homepage (www.civl.port.ac.uk/comp_prog/cntower/index.html). Provides history, interesting facts, and a photo gallery of the tower.

About the Author

Meg Greene is a writer and historian with a particular interest in late-nineteenth- and early-twentieth-century architecture. She has a BS in history from Lindenwood College in St. Charles, Missouri; an MA in history from the University of Nebraska–Omaha; and an MS in historic preservation from the University of Vermont. Ms. Greene makes her home in Virginia.